GREAT HITTERS OF THE NEGRO LEAGUES

By Paul Hoblin

Content Consultant
Raymond Doswell, Ed.D.
Curator, Negro Leagues Baseball Museum

Published by ABDO Publishing Company, PO Box 398166, Minneapolis,
MN 55439. Copyright © 2013 by Abdo Consulting Group, Inc. International
copyrights reserved in all countries. No part of this book may be reproduced
in any form without written permission from the publisher. SportsZone™ is
a trademark and logo of ABDO Publishing Company.

Printed in the United States of America,
North Mankato, Minnesota
052012
902012

Editor: Chrös McDougall
Series Designer: Emily Love

Photo Credits

Mark Rucker/Transcendental Graphics, Getty Images, cover, 52; AP Images,
8, 17, 20; Transcendental Graphics/Getty Images, 11; Negro Leagues
Baseball Museum, 13, 14, 23, 25, 31, 32, 39, 44, 47, 51; National Baseball
Hall of Fame Library, Cooperstown, NY, 28, 36, 41; Bettmann/Corbis/AP
Images, 49, 57

Design elements: Patricia Hofmeester/Shutterstock Images; Bryan Solomon/
Shutterstock Images

Library of Congress Cataloging-in-Publication Data

Hoblin, Paul.
  Great hitters of the Negro leagues / Paul Hoblin.
    p. cm. -- (The Negro baseball leagues)
  Includes bibliographical references.
  ISBN 978-1-61783-507-0
  1. Negro leagues--History--Juvenile literature. 2. African American baseball
players--History--Juvenile literature. I. Title.
  GV875.N35H63 2012
  796.357'64--dc23
                      2012010837

TABLE OF CONTENTS

INTRODUCTION

Baseball has been called America's pastime. Yet the professional sport has not always been open to everyone. Many of the game's most revered players—from sluggers Babe Ruth and Ty Cobb to pitchers Christy Mathewson and Walter Johnson—played during an era when black players were unofficially barred from Major League Baseball (MLB). So, with little other choice, the black players created their own leagues—the Negro Leagues.

Blacks began playing baseball during the mid-1800s, not long after the sport was founded. But from the beginning, they faced discrimination. In fact, many of the early all-black games were between teams made up of slaves. Black players did make inroads into organized baseball later in the century. Some even made it into the major leagues. But by 1900, an unofficial color line was drawn, preventing black players from playing on the biggest stage.

The Negro National League (NNL) was founded in 1920 as the first successfully organized Negro League. Other Negro Leagues later formed in the eastern and southern

United States. And some teams, not in any leagues, simply traveled the country performing in exhibition games.

Life could be very hard for the Negro Leagues teams. Blacks did not have the same rights as whites at the time. Hotels sometimes refused to house them. Restaurants refused to serve them. Pay was low compared to that of the major leaguers. Discrimination was just a fact of life.

Although the Negro Leagues were largely unknown to whites, the black community viewed them as success stories. The big games attracted a who's who of black society. And today, the greatest Negro Leagues players are rightfully recognized in the National Baseball Hall of Fame.

The Negro Leagues were at their height in the early 1940s, when many of the top white players were away fighting in World War II. MLB's color line was finally shattered in 1947, when Jackie Robinson played his first game for the Brooklyn Dodgers. Full integration soon followed, and the Negro Leagues faded away by the 1960s. But the exciting stories of legendary players of the Negro Leagues live on, reminding most of the world what it had missed out on during the early 1900s.

JOHN HENRY "POP" LLOYD

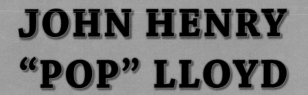

John Henry Lloyd retired from baseball at the age of 58. By then he was both respected and loved by everyone who cared about black baseball. In fact, everyone who knew him called him "Pop." It was a nickname that honored Lloyd's status as one of the Negro Leagues' founding fathers.

Of course, Lloyd was not born with either his reputation or his nickname. Both had to be earned over a lifetime of playing baseball.

BEFORE HE WAS POP

Lloyd was born on April 25, 1884, in Palatka, Florida. He was still very young when his father died. After Lloyd's mother remarried, he was sent to live with his grandmother. Florida was segregated at the time, which meant life could be very hard for blacks. Like most black kids in Florida, Lloyd began working full-time before he had finished elementary school. During the day he had a job as a store delivery boy and then as a railroad porter. Afterward, and during any free time he could find, Lloyd played baseball on various all-black ballclubs.

In 1905, Lloyd moved from a sandlot team in Jacksonville,

WILLARD BROWN

Perhaps the greatest slugger of the 1940s was Willard Brown. His most popular nickname was Ese Hombre. *Ese Hombre* means "that man," which is how Puerto Rican fans described him as he walked up to the plate while playing winter ball in that country. He hit so many home runs, the fans would say, "Here comes that man again." In 1947 the St. Louis Browns of MLB signed him. However, they released him after only 21 games. During his short time in the majors, he faced his share of racism. He once hit a home run with a teammate's bat. The teammate immediately broke the bat so Brown could never use it again. Brown was inducted into the National Baseball Hall of Fame in 2006.

Florida, to the semiprofessional Macon Acmes in Georgia. It was there that Lloyd proved both his toughness and his creativity. Like many all-black teams, the Acmes did not have much money. They could not even afford to buy a catcher's mask. Lloyd, then a catcher, did his best without one. But in the third inning of one particular game, an opposing batter fouled a ball off Lloyd's left eye. The eye quickly became so swollen that he could not see out of it. Lloyd spit on his finger, rubbed the eye, and said he could keep catching.

In the seventh inning, another foul ball slammed into his right eye. Before leaving the game, Lloyd apologized to the other players. "Gentlemen," he said. "I guess I'll have to quit, I can't see the ball." The next day he showed up wearing a wire basket on his head and resumed his catching duties.

POP IN HIS PRIME

Lloyd began as a catcher, but he went on to play other positions. He was best known as a shortstop. In his prime, Lloyd was perhaps the best infielder in baseball. He joined the all-black Cuban X Giants in 1906. They were one of the top

John Henry "Pop" Lloyd was one of black baseball's pioneers. He was inducted into the National Baseball Hall of Fame in 1977.

Negro Leagues teams at the time. Lloyd made an early impact. He hit a game-winning double in his first game.

The Cuban X Giants were not the only Giants team Lloyd played for. Within the next five years he switched from the Cuban X Giants to the Philadelphia Giants to the Leland Giants to the Lincoln Giants to the Chicago American Giants.

The reason for all these moves was simple. "Wherever the money was," Lloyd said, "that's where I was."

This way of life was not considered greedy or disloyal at the time. Even in the major leagues, baseball players were paid much less than they are today. And while MLB was a major sport in the United States, the Negro Leagues were largely unknown. As such, many Negro Leagues teams struggled

DICK LUNDY

After John Henry "Pop" Lloyd, the next great black shortstop was Dick Lundy. Lundy was born in 1898 and entered his prime during the 1920s. He was a consistent hitter from both sides of the plate. However, Lundy often ignored his current contract in order to sign a better one with another team. In 1920, he signed three different contracts. The teams eventually brought him to court to decide who had the right to claim him. In addition to his hitting abilities, Lundy was known for being almost completely silent. He would rarely say a word during a game. That is, until he became a manager and had to give instructions.

Dick Lundy, *back left*, and Pop Lloyd, *back second from left*, played for the Almendares Baseball Club in Havana, Cuba, around 1927.

to make money. Black ballplayers often had to switch teams in order to make a decent living.

All this moving had little effect on Lloyd's quality of play. Much of his career came before the first NNL was formed in 1920. Although blacks could not play in the white major and minor leagues, they often played exhibition games against the white teams. Lloyd shined against both black and white teams.

Lloyd was still playing for the Lincoln Giants in 1913. His team pummeled the Philadelphia Phillies by a score of 9–2. Lloyd was so impressive in his prime that some began calling him "the black Wagner." Honus Wagner was considered the greatest shortstop in the game. The nickname was meant to be a great compliment.

WILLIE WELLS

Willie Wells was another great Negro Leagues shortstop. But unlike Pop Lloyd or Dick Lundy, Wells did not have a great arm. Instead, he used his speed to cut the ball off and get rid of it quickly. According to Walter "Buck" Leonard, Wells's arm never got him into trouble. "He could always get his man at first," Leonard recalled. Wells was also known for his skill at catching pop flies and fly balls over his head. That allowed the outfielders to stay farther back and prevent extra-base hits.

Still, Wagner said he was the one flattered by the nickname. "I am honored to have John Lloyd called the Black Wagner," he said. "It is a privilege to have been compared with him."

Indeed, Lloyd was talented in all aspects of baseball. As a hitter, he hit for high averages. He also hit with power. In fact, he batted in the important fourth spot for some of the best teams of the era. As a fielder, he studied hitters and pounced on ground balls. His hands were so sure and so strong that in Cuba they called him *El Cuchara*. That meant "the Shovel." The Cubans knew Lloyd from his many years playing winter baseball there.

THE END OF A BASEBALL LIFE

Lloyd continued to play professional baseball until 1931. He played semipro baseball for many years after that. He also became a manager.

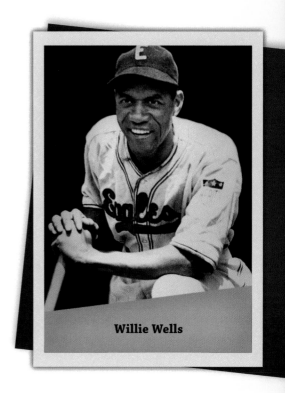

Willie Wells

Those who played for Lloyd appreciated both his kindness and his confidence in them. Lloyd was a fierce competitor. But that competitiveness did not translate into yelling or cussing. Even as a player, legend has it that the harshest words he ever spoke were "Dad burn!" That was a Southern phrase to express frustration.

His gentleness and gift for storytelling made him a favorite with school kids as well. Lloyd worked as a janitor at a school after finally retiring from baseball. Between classes, kids would flock to him. They asked him to talk about his experiences in the Negro Leagues. The kids were so drawn to his stories that they would sometimes be late for class.

Shortstop Pop Lloyd was considered one of the greatest baseball players of the early 1900s.

Lloyd would have to pick them up by the shoulders and set them down in their classrooms.

In 1947, Jackie Robinson broke the color barrier in MLB. Lloyd had long since stopped playing by then. But two years later, a $150,000 stadium was named after him in Atlantic City, New Jersey. It was a fitting tribute to a man who dedicated his life to the diamond.

THE GIANTS

Pop Lloyd was one of many Negro Leagues players to play on a team called the Giants. That is because there were many Negro Leagues teams that went by the name. Negro Leaguer John "Buck" O'Neil said the name was meant to help fans identify when all-black teams were coming to town. At the time, some newspapers refused to print pictures of black players, so it was hard to tell if traveling teams were black.

OSCAR CHARLESTON

During his playing days, Oscar Charleston was often called "the black Ty Cobb." Cobb was a Hall of Fame outfielder in MLB. He played 22 seasons with the Detroit Tigers from 1905 until 1926 before joining the Philadelphia Athletics for two more. When he finally retired, Cobb's 4,189 career hits were an MLB record. He was one of the major leagues' best base stealers as well.

Cobb was one of baseball's brightest stars of the early 1900s. Charleston did not share his glory. The Negro Leagues were very

Oscar Charleston was often compared to MLB star Ty Cobb. Both were great hitters, fast, and had bad tempers.

much in the background of mainstream society during his career, which lasted from 1915 to 1954. The Negro Leagues' organization and record keeping were also inferior to MLB's. As such, many of Charleston's statistics were lost or perhaps never even recorded.

To those who saw Charleston play, however, the comparisons to Cobb were reasonable. Like Cobb, Charleston was really fast. While in the army, he ran a 220-yard dash in 23 seconds. Both ballplayers were also great hitters. They each hit better than .350 over the course of their careers.

But perhaps the greatest similarity between these two men was their temper. Cobb was well known for his mean streak. He would sharpen his cleats in the dugout so opposing infielders would fear getting spiked. Unlike Cobb, Charleston was well liked by the other players. But that did not stop him from getting into fights with them.

Charleston brawled with players, umpires, owners, scouts, policemen, and armed soldiers during his career. According to one story, he even got in a quarrel with a member of the Ku Klux Klan. The Klan is an organization whose members believe whites are better than other races. Charleston pulled off the Klansman's hood so he could not hide his face. Then Charleston dared the man to continue degrading him because of his race. The Klansman left Charleston alone after that.

GROW UP

Charleston's fierceness helped him survive his time in the military. He was born in 1896 in Indianapolis, Indiana.

Charleston was the seventh of 11 kids. Around age 15, he ran off to join the armed forces.

Charleston returned to Indianapolis approximately four years later, in 1915. He was just 19 years old. However, Charleston had grown into a 6-foot-tall, barrel-chested man. He was both blazingly fast and dangerously strong.

REPRESENTING THE UNITED STATES

When the United States entered World War I in 1917, several black men joined the military. Among them were Negro League stars such as Wilber "Bullet Joe" Rogan, Dave Malarcher, and Jimmy Lyons. Spottswood Poles, one of the fastest and most skilled players of his era, earned five battle stars and a Purple Heart for his service to the country.

However, these black ballplayers were not treated as heroes when they returned to the United States. Because of the color of their skin, they still could not eat at many restaurants, drink at many drinking fountains, or sleep at many hotels. Things had not improved much when World War II broke out a couple decades later. Those who became soldiers were faced with racist commanders and comrades on a daily basis. While first baseman John "Buck" O'Neil was in the navy, he was told he could have been an officer—if only he was white.

Just like the black ballplayers who returned from World War I, Negro Leaguers returning home after World War II found themselves once again sitting in the back of buses and paying for gas at stations that would not allow them to use the bathroom.

Oscar Charleston, *far left*, was one of five future Hall of Famers on the 1935 Pittsburgh Crawfords. Many consider that to be the best Negro Leagues team ever.

Charleston began playing baseball for the all-black Indianapolis ABCs that year. Almost right away he got into his first fight with an umpire. Afterward Charleston apologized for his behavior in a letter to his fans. The incident, he said, had been "highly unwise."

Charleston's talent emerged as quickly as his readiness to fight. In 1916, the ABCs beat the Chicago American Giants in a black championship series (the first official Negro World Series was not held until 1924). Charleston was already one of the stars of black baseball. In 1921, he led the NNL in stolen bases, batting average, triples, and home runs.

Many considered Charleston to be the best player in the Negro Leagues throughout the 1920s. Even as his youth and speed vanished in the 1930s, Charleston remained one of the most feared hitters in the game.

Charleston later became a player/manager and then just a manager. Jimmy Crutchfield was a member of the 1936 Pittsburgh Crawfords. Charleston was the team's player/manager. Crutchfield remembers playing a game against an MLB all-star team. According to Crutchfield, Charleston hit pop flies in his first two at-bats. When he came back to the dugout, Charleston complained that it was boring to bat with no one on base. The next time up, Charleston got his wish. Two of his teammates had managed to reach base. Charleston stepped into the batter's box and ripped a double off the wall.

This was not the only time Charleston experienced success against white all-star teams. His overall batting average during these exhibition games was .318. He also hit 11 home runs in 53 games. Dizzy Dean was a white Hall of Fame pitcher who

LOUIS SANTOP

During the 1910s and 1920s, Louis Santop was perhaps the biggest draw in black baseball. Like baseball legend Babe Ruth supposedly did, Santop once "called his shot" in a game. A heckler bet him a dollar that he would strike out. Santop pointed to the right field fence and said he was going to hit a home run. Needless to say, Santop went home with an extra dollar in his pocket.

starred for the St. Louis Cardinals. He pitched against Charleston in an exhibition, though, and was amazed by Charleston's power. When Charleston was up, Dean said all a pitcher could do was hope he did not "get a hold of one and send it out of the park."

It was also this power that separated Charleston from Cobb. Though he was called "the black Ty Cobb," Charleston was far more likely to hit a home run than his white counterpart. John "Buck" O'Neil later became an ambassador for the Negro Leagues, traveling around and sharing stories. According to O'Neil, the only ballplayer who could accurately be compared to Charleston was another black man—Willie Mays.

Mays played briefly in the Negro Leagues, but most of his career came after MLB's integration. Some people consider Mays to be the greatest all-around player in MLB history.

**Oscar Charleston is considered one of baseball's greatest
all-around players.**

Of course, Mays would have never had the chance to play in the
majors if great Negro Leaguers such as Oscar Charleston had
not fought their way through the color line on his behalf.

3

JAMES "COOL PAPA" BELL

There were many words to describe James "Cool Papa" Bell. Switch-hitter. All-Star. Hall of Famer. But the first word used by those who saw him play was *fast*. Cool Papa Bell, many contemporaries say, was the fastest man in baseball history.

Bell was known to run faster than routine groundballs and average bunts. Infielders automatically moved closer to the plate when Bell stepped into the batter's box. Otherwise, they knew they would not have a shot at throwing him out at first.

James "Cool Papa" Bell was known as one of the fastest baseball players of all time.

But Bell's quickness went beyond minor defensive adjustments. His speed was the stuff of legend. One time, Jimmy Crutchfield claimed Bell hit a ground ball up the middle that rolled into Bell as he slid into second base. Pitching great Leroy "Satchel" Paige disputed this story. He said Bell did not hit himself with his own groundball. Instead, he hit himself with his own *line drive*!

In 1936, black track star Jesse Owens won four gold medals at the Olympic Games. Owens came home from Berlin, Germany, as a national hero. However, even his Olympic medals could not shield him from discrimination. Many supposed business deals turned out to be publicity stunts, and Owens was left scraping for money.

One of the ways Owens earned a living after the Olympics was through track-and-field exhibitions. Shortly after the 1936 Games, the Pittsburgh Crawfords hired Owens to race around the bases as pregame entertainment. Sometimes Owens would outrun horses. Other times he would give Crawfords players a 10-yard head start. Yet Owens always passed them on the base paths.

Bell was on the Crawfords at the time. But for some reason he was never asked to race Owens. Negro Leaguer John "Buck" O'Neil thought that Owens was afraid he would lose. Paige was certain of it. "Jesse Owens would have looked like he was walking," Paige said.

FASTER THAN THE SPEED OF LIGHT

The most famous Cool Papa Bell story also involved Paige. For decades, Paige told people a story about Bell's speed. He said that Bell was so fast he could flip off a light switch and be under the covers before the bedroom went dark. And it turns out the story was true—more or less.

One night Bell and Paige were rooming together in a hotel. Bell flipped the light switch to go to bed. However, there was some sort of electrical short. The light would delay for a few

"COOL PAPA"

James "Cool Papa" Bell was born in 1903 in Starkville, Mississippi. He was known mostly for his speed when he was inducted into the National Baseball Hall of Fame in 1974. But he began his Negro Leagues career in 1922 as a very capable left-handed pitcher. However, arm trouble forced Bell to move to the outfield in 1924.

It was during that time when Bell earned his famous nickname. The St. Louis Stars' manager was impressed by how "cool" Bell was under pressure. So he decided to call him "Cool Papa," adding the second part for effect.

Bell was a Negro Leagues star for nearly three decades after that. Then he worked several years as a custodian. The former speedster lived until 1991. Although Bell never got an opportunity to play in the major leagues, he lived long enough to see himself and several contemporaries honored in the Hall of Fame.

27

Cool Papa Bell of the Homestead Grays slides into third base during a 1932 Negro Leagues game in Washington DC.

seconds before going out. Paige was not in the room yet, and Bell got an idea.

Later that night, Bell bet Paige $50 that he was faster than the speed of light. Paige thought he was about to win easy money. But then Bell flipped the switch. The light stalled, and Bell "proved" that he was indeed faster than light leaving a bulb.

STAYING SPEEDY

There is no doubt that many legends about Bell's speed are greatly exaggerated. Still, his title as the fastest man in baseball holds a lot of truth. Bell was 45 years old and had played professional baseball for a quarter century by 1948. Yet his legs remained a blur on the base paths.

MR. VERSATILE

Martin Dihigo, a Cuban, played in the Negro Leagues as well as in many other countries. He was known to be excellent at every position. Also called "El Maestro," Dihigo was even versatile at the plate. He could hit well from either the right side or the left. In the 1935 East-West All-Star Game, Dihigo started in center field, hit third in the lineup, and then came in as a relief pitcher. His career began in 1923 and continued into the 1950s.

That year he was playing against a white all-star team in Los Angeles. Bell found himself on first base. In addition to being fast, Bell was also smart. That day, he noticed that the pitcher had a habit of staring at first base exactly once before delivering the pitch home. Bell waited for the pitcher to look at first base. Then he waited for the pitcher to look away. That is when Bell took off for second.

DOUBLE DUTY

Ted "Double Duty" Radcliffe was another versatile Negro Leaguer. His claim to fame was playing both pitcher and catcher, sometimes on the same day. Radcliffe played on some of the greatest teams in black baseball. Among them were the St. Louis Stars, the Homestead Grays, and the Pittsburgh Crawfords. He appeared in six Negro Leagues East-West All-Star games—three as a pitcher, and three as a catcher.

The batter bunted the ball as Bell raced around second base. The catcher saw Bell streaking for third. He abandoned home plate to cover third base. When Bell saw that no one was covering home, he dodged the catcher's tag and raced for the plate.

Even though he was nearing the end of his career, Bell had just accomplished the seemingly impossible. He had cruised safely from first to home on a bunt, despite the fact that no one on the opposing team had committed an error.

MORE THAN A SPEEDSTER

Bell was deservedly known for his great speed. But he was much more than just a very fast player. He was also a great hitter who averaged better than .400 on several occasions. In addition, he was a great manager who tutored future MLB greats such as Ernie Banks and Jackie Robinson.

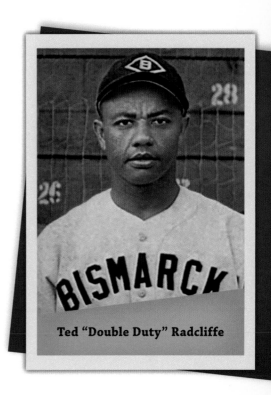

Ted "Double Duty" Radcliffe

Off the diamond, Bell was most appreciated for his compassion for other black baseball players. Bell was still a great hitter after Robinson broke the MLB color line in 1947. In fact, as the Negro Leagues regular season drew to a close, Bell found himself atop the leader board for batting average. But Bell intentionally forfeited the batting title to Monte Irvin. He hoped that Irvin's batting title would catch the eye of an MLB team. Indeed, Irvin later became a star player for the New York Giants.

Bell finally retired in 1950, after nearly 30 years in the Negro Leagues. Although he played during the era of integration, Bell never had the opportunity to play in the major leagues. Bell claimed to have no regrets about that. He said his greatest thrill "was when they opened the door in the majors to black players."

FROM BASEBALL TO BUCKETS

The Negro League Baseball Players Association describes Cool Papa Bell as having the "build of a high school point guard." But Clarence "Fats" Jenkins really did play hoops. During the baseball off-season he played basketball for the New York Renaissance. It was an all-black basketball squad established in New York during the 1920s. Make no mistake about Jenkins's nickname, though. "Fats" was a childhood nickname that stuck with him into adulthood. Jenkins was actually quite skinny.

Following his playing days, Cool Papa Bell became a successful baseball manager.

4

WALTER "BUCK" LEONARD

It took Walter "Buck" Leonard a long time to become a Negro Leagues baseball player. In fact, early in his life the idea that Leonard could make a living playing baseball must have seemed impossible.

Born September 8, 1907, in Rocky Mount, North Carolina, Leonard had a hard upbringing. As a young boy, he was once arrested for simply trying to watch a baseball game between two white teams. When he was 12 his father died during a flu epidemic. After that, Leonard was forced to work at a hosiery mill making stockings and at a railroad station as a shoeshine boy. Leonard was out of school by age 16. His town did not have a high school for black kids, and his family needed whatever money he could earn. He put brake cylinders on boxcars at the railroad station until he was 25. Then he lost his job due to the Great Depression.

It was only then that Leonard decided to give pro baseball a try. He had been playing for a semipro team in North Carolina before that. A year after he lost his job, Leonard signed with the Homestead Grays. The Pittsburgh-area team was one of the most successful in the Negro Leagues. That success would continue during Leonard's 17 seasons there.

It was rare for a Negro Leagues player to stay on one team for a long time. But first baseman Leonard and catcher

GETTING A DEGREE

Opportunities were limited for blacks when Walter "Buck" Leonard was growing up in Rocky Mount, North Carolina. The town was segregated, so blacks and whites could not go to school together. In fact, blacks could not go to school at all, because Rocky Mount did not have high school for black students. Leonard still earned his high school degree. However, it was not until he was 52.

Josh Gibson were cornerstones for the Grays for many years. Together they formed what some called the most feared hitting duo in all of black baseball. The two men were often compared to white stars Babe Ruth and Lou Gehrig of the New York Yankees. They led the Yankees to four World Series from 1926 to 1934, winning three of them. However, some who played with Gibson and Leonard thought the comparison was misleading. As great as Ruth and Gehrig were, these players claimed Gibson and Leonard were even better. Together they led the Grays to four Negro World Series and won two.

For his part, Leonard was almost certainly a better fielding first baseman than Gehrig. He had a great ability for digging out throws in the dirt. He also had a strong, accurate arm. Leonard was spectacular at the plate as well. Leonard's career batting average was .341. From 1936 to 1943, he hit at least 34 home runs per season (counting exhibitions).

"If he'd gotten the chance to play in the major leagues," said Hall of Famer Monte Irvin, "they might have called Lou Gehrig 'The White Buck Leonard.'"

Walter "Buck" Leonard starred for the famous Homestead Grays for 17 seasons, many alongside Josh Gibson.

CLOSING IN ON THE COLOR LINE

Leonard's Grays won nine consecutive NNL championships (1937 to 1945). They added one more championship in 1948. The last pennant was perhaps the most impressive. The year before, Gibson unexpectedly died. Still, Leonard won the batting title with a .395 average. He also tied for the league lead in home runs with 13. He was 40 years old but remained one of the most dangerous hitters in the game.

Two years earlier, in 1946, the Brooklyn Dodgers signed Jackie Robinson to play for their top minor league team. He debuted with the Dodgers the next spring. Team president Branch Rickey was responsible for signing Robinson.

"TURKEY"

Buck Leonard made hitting a baseball look easy. But as Norman "Turkey" Stearnes proved, being a great hitter does not have to mean being an effortless hitter. Stearnes got his nickname because of the way he flapped his arms wildly as he ran the bases. He was also called "the Gobbler." And that was not the only strange thing about him. Stearnes was obsessed with hitting. He was so obsessed that he kept his bats in violin cases and carried them around wherever he went. Stearnes was even known to talk to his bats. After one game, he turned to his 34-inch bat and said, "I used you and only hit the ball up against the fence." Turning his attention to his 35-inch bat, he lamented, "If I had used you, I would have hit the ball over the fence."

In 1948, Rickey made it known that he was interested in signing Leonard too. For reasons that never became public, Rickey did not follow through with his plans. So Leonard continued to play for the Grays.

Norman "Turkey" Stearnes

That was not the first time a MLB team had taken a look at Leonard. In 1938, almost a decade before Robinson broke the color line, Washington Senators owner Clark Griffith invited Leonard and Josh Gibson into his office. He was apparently interested in signing the players, but said it was not the right time.

Griffith's interest in the black stars was understandable. The Senators were almost always at the bottom of the standings. Gibson and Leonard, meanwhile, were in their prime as players. Their presence in the Senators' lineup could have drastically improved the ballclub.

In addition, the Grays played many of their home games at the Senators' stadium. It is likely that Griffith was watching

39

THE OTHER BUCK

There was another excellent first baseman in the 1930s who shared Leonard's nickname: John "Buck" O'Neil. Though not as good as Leonard, O'Neil was an all-star for the Kansas City Monarchs. The Monarchs were another superb Negro Leagues team. They even beat the Homestead Grays in the 1942 Negro World Series. Like Leonard, O'Neil later became a great ambassador of the Negro Leagues. O'Neil shared his memories and stories with whoever would listen. In 1994 director Ken Burns made a documentary called *Baseball*. It featured O'Neil's commentary concerning black baseball in the first half of the twentieth century.

out his office window as Gibson and Leonard performed some of their greatest feats. Their presence would also make the Senators more appealing for black fans. However, Griffith's interest never went beyond that. Baseball waited another nine years to get rid of its color line.

LONG RESPECTED

Over his long career, Leonard was not only feared by opponents but respected. He liked to sit in the hotel lobby between games and work on crossword puzzles. Young players would often seek him out. Leonard would offer advice and encouragement before they left for nightclubs. He then resumed filling out his puzzles.

40

Large crowds came to see Buck Leonard (4) and Josh Gibson lead the Homestead Grays. The Grays were one of the most successful Negro Leagues teams.

In 1952, Leonard was once again offered a chance to play in the big leagues. Bill Veeck owned the St. Louis Browns. He wanted Leonard on his team. Leonard turned him down, though. By that point, Leonard said he was too old to play in the majors. He did not want his declining abilities to "hurt the chances of those who might follow."

Even after Leonard retired as a player, he spent the rest of his life sharing his memories about the Negro Leagues. In 1972, he was finally inducted into baseball's Hall of Fame. He is remembered as one of the Negro Leagues' greatest ambassadors, an invaluable resource to both historians and fans, and one of the best players to ever play the game.

JOSH GIBSON

Of all the great hitters in the Negro Leagues, Josh Gibson is widely regarded as the greatest. The length of his home runs was mythical even in his own time. Once, it was reported that Gibson hit a hard line drive. It barely cleared the pitcher's head. Then it supposedly kept on going past the infield, past the outfield, and over the fence. Another time, Gibson hit one so far and so hard that he knocked a speaker off the stadium's roof.

Gibson's Homestead Grays played some games at Griffith Stadium in Washington DC.

Gibson was known to blast balls into trees that stood behind center field. That was more than 500 feet from home plate.

Then there is the story about a home run Gibson hit in Pittsburgh. The ball blasted off Gibson's bat with such force that fans could not swivel their heads in time to follow it through the air. The players searched for the ball. But their efforts were fruitless. The umpire finally decided it must have landed on the other side of the fence. Gibson was awarded a home run.

Gibson's team was playing the next day in Philadelphia. A ball supposedly dropped out of the sky and landed in the center fielder's glove. The umpire must have heard about the missing ball from the day before. He pointed at Gibson and said, "Yer out—yesterday in Pittsburgh!"

THE BEST, BUT NOT THE FIRST

Josh Gibson was the best home-run hitter in black baseball. But there were other power hitters who came before him. One of the first was Grant "Home Run" Johnson. He played on several teams before 1920. In 1910 Johnson was a member of the Havana Reds. That was a Cuban team that competed against major league squads. Playing against Ty Cobb's Detroit Tigers, Johnson hit over .400.

Catcher Josh Gibson developed into the Negro Leagues' greatest power hitter.

Some of these stories clearly stretch the truth. But the point they convey is true enough: Gibson spent his career hitting massive home runs. To those who watched him play, Gibson was no mere mortal. He was superhuman—a ballplayer who used a simple compact swing to crush baseballs into the stratosphere.

MOVING NORTH

Gibson was born in 1911 in Buena Vista, Georgia. When he was 12, his family moved to Pittsburgh. Gibson's father hoped there would be more opportunities for his children there. The South was still officially segregated at the time. Blacks had to use different public facilities from whites. It was also legal for places such as restaurants to discriminate based on race.

There was some racism in the North, of course. But Gibson was forever grateful for the move. "The greatest gift Dad gave me," he said, "was getting me out of the South."

It was in Pittsburgh that Gibson fell in love with baseball. He was always on the lookout for the next game. He loved both to play and to simply watch the game. Gibson routinely roller-skated six miles (9.7 km) to a ballpark in Bellevue in order to attend an organized ballgame.

Soon, Gibson was the first one picked during pickup games in the community. He joined his first organized baseball team when he was 16 years old. By then he was over six feet tall and weighed more than 200 pounds. Much of that weight was in muscle. Only two years later, Gibson became a professional baseball player.

IT PAYS TO BE A FAN

On July 25, 1930, the Homestead Grays were playing against the Kansas City Monarchs. The Grays' catcher, William "Buck" Ewing, split his finger open and had to leave the game. This was a night game, and bad lighting led to Ewing's injury.

The Monarchs' owner had come up with a portable lighting system that he brought with him on the road. These lights were both creative and revolutionary. They allowed baseball fans who worked during the day to attend Negro League games. That allowed the teams to make more money. It would not take long for MLB teams to put lights in their stadiums, too.

Still, not all the players liked the lights. That was largely because the lights did not work very well. The pitcher that night was the great "Smoky Joe" Williams. He could barely make out Ewing's fingers as the catcher signaled for different pitches. Williams threw a fastball when Ewing was expecting a curve. The result was Ewing's split finger.

The manager asked backup catcher Vic Harris to put on the gear. But Harris refused. He was not going to try to catch

THE BEST BACKSTOP IN BLACK BASEBALL

Over the course of his career, Josh Gibson improved a great deal defensively. However, everyone seems to agree that the best defensive catcher in the Negro Leagues was Raleigh "Biz" Mackey. Mackey began his professional career in 1918. He was still playing into the 1940s. He was in his 50s when he finally called it quits. Mackey's arm was so good that he could throw the ball harder to second while still on his knees than most catchers could throw it standing up. And he was no slouch at the plate, either. During the 1925 Negro World Series, Mackey led his ballclub with a .375 average.

Williams's flameball in the dark, he said.

Raleigh "Biz" Mackey

There was a delay in the game as the Grays tried to find another catcher. Word arrived that Gibson was sitting in the stands. Fans were aware of Gibson through his semipro team. Stories had spread about the 18-year-old's incredible power at the plate. Crowds were beginning to flock to watch him play.

That night, the Grays' owner asked Gibson if he would finish the game behind the plate. Gibson agreed. Everyone waited for him to descend from the stands and put on the mask. He never played semipro ball again.

A NEGRO LEAGUES SENSATION

Gibson's skills as a catcher were questionable when he first entered the league. His hands were unsure. His arm was unreliable. He had a lifelong difficulty with foul pops. Yet those who were at that first professional game said Gibson did not drop a single pitch. His defensive skills improved greatly over the course of his career.

Most agreed that he was an excellent backstop by the time he retired. But in the meantime, no one worried too much about his weaknesses behind the plate. They were too distracted by his production at the plate.

Gibson hit what was perhaps his most famous home run as an 18-year-old. He was in Yankee Stadium in New York. The ballpark was also known as the House That Ruth Built. That is because the popularity of Yankees legend Babe Ruth helped lead to its construction.

Gibson soon acquired the nickname "the black Babe Ruth." Former Negro Leaguer John "Buck" O'Neil said that the ball sounded different when it left Ruth's and Gibson's bats. In fact, that is how O'Neil encountered Gibson for the first time. O'Neil was in the locker room when he heard Gibson taking batting practice. He was so excited that he ran out wearing only his underwear to watch Gibson hit.

Many considered Ruth to be the greatest power hitter in MLB history. Others have since surpassed his records, but nobody in Ruth's time came close. Still, for all his power, Ruth never hit a ball out of Yankee Stadium. But that is exactly what Gibson did as an 18-year-old. At least, according to legend.

Josh Gibson is tagged out at home plate during an East-West All-Star Game in Chicago.

Gibson was facing New York Lincoln Giants pitcher Connie Rector in the ninth inning. Gibson launched a ball that cleared the fence and the bullpen. Then the story gets hazy.

Bill Holland played third base for the Lincoln Giants. He said the ball finally came down at the back of the bullpen. Larry Brown, New York's catcher, said the ball bounced off the top of the back wall. That would be a mere two feet from leaving the stadium. But William "Judy" Johnson, the Grays' manager,

"KICK, MULE!"

George "Mule" Suttles was one of the Negro Leagues' best home-run hitters. Suttles once hit a ball so far while playing in Havana, Cuba, that a marker was erected to mark the spot where it landed. His nickname was due to his strength. He is said to have wielded a 50-ounce bat. His teammates would often yell, "Kick, Mule!" as he got ready for the next pitch.

insisted that it *did* leave the stadium.

Nobody knows for certain where the ball landed. But what is certain is that Gibson's home run was extremely long. Some believe it was the longest homer ever hit at Yankee Stadium.

Unless, that is, Gibson's second most famous home run was even longer. In 1934, he hit another ball that soared over the bullpen. According to Jack Marshall of the Chicago American Giants, it too kept on soaring out of the stadium.

MIND-NUMBING NUMBERS

The length of Gibson's home runs was impressive. The number of home runs he hit was impressive too. Many MLB statistics became skewed during the 1990s and early 2000s, when some players used illegal performance-enhancing drugs. Before that era, the MLB single-season home-run record was Roger Maris's

61. And before that, Ruth's 60 homers in 1927 stood as the MLB record.

Gibson exceeded those totals on numerous occasions. He hit 75 home runs in 1931. In 1934, the total was 69. And in 1936, at the height of his baseball powers, Gibson clobbered an astonishing 84 home runs in 170 games.

A career total is difficult to determine, and even more difficult to evaluate. Some say Gibson hit more than 900 homers. Others point out that many of his home runs were hit against weak competition.

George "Mule" Suttles

In order to survive, Negro Leagues players and teams had to do a lot of barnstorming. This meant they went from town to town playing semipro and local teams that had far less talent and skill than they did. On the other hand, others point out that the major league players were playing against weaker competition as well. After all, they did not have to face the top black players.

Leroy "Satchel" Paige, *left*, and Josh Gibson chat before a 1941 game. They are considered two of the greatest Negro Leaguers of all time.

MAKING ENDS MEET

Pitcher Leroy "Satchel" Paige was one of the Negro Leagues' biggest draws. Gibson was another. Both players did their fair share of team-switching during their careers. In 15 years, Gibson went from the Homestead Grays to the Pittsburgh Crawfords and then back to the Grays. In 1937, he traveled to the Dominican Republic to play for dictator Rafael Trujillo's all-star team. Then he returned to the Grays for a couple seasons before jumping his contract and heading for Mexico.

Like most other Negro Leagues players, Gibson's reason for switching teams was money. MLB players were paid enough to make a good living. However, even the best Negro Leaguers could not afford to choose loyalty over a higher salary.

DEATH OF A LEGEND

Gibson returned to the Grays in 1942. However, it was around this time that he started to suffer from very bad headaches. On New Year's Day of 1943, Gibson fell into a coma. It lasted for a day and left him in the hospital more than a week. Gibson had a brain tumor, the doctors said. An operation was needed to remove it.

But Gibson refused surgery. He was afraid of losing most of his brain function. So he endured the headaches. Gibson also had developed bad knees. But he continued to crush baseballs for the Grays. Statistics from the 1940s reveal no dip in his production. He was still the greatest hitter in black baseball. He was still Josh Gibson.

The Grays won nine straight pennants from 1937 to 1945. Gibson continued to be a mainstay in the middle of their lineup. But the headaches were getting worse. By the winter of 1946, Gibson suffered from repeated blackouts. On January 20, 1947, the great ballplayer died of a massive stroke. He was only 35 years old.

There are conflicting reports about how and where Gibson died. Some say he was in a movie theater when it happened. Others that he was at home in bed.

In the version about his dying in bed, Gibson entered his home and announced to his mother that he was about to have a stroke. She assured him that he was mistaken, but brought him to his bed anyway. Gibson's family gathered around him. Gibson then asked his brother to bring all his trophies into the room.

When his brother returned, he found Gibson laughing and talking with all the others. All of a sudden he sat up and opened his mouth as if to talk. Then he lay back down, and never got up again.

WHAT HE'S WORTH

Like many Negro Leagues players, Josh Gibson struggled to earn a living in black baseball. Joe DiMaggio was one of MLB's best players during the 1940s. He made between $30,000 and $40,000 per year for much of his career. Walter Johnson, one of the all-time great major league pitchers, said that Gibson was worth $200,000. "Too bad this Gibson is a colored fellow," Johnson added.

LOVE OF THE GAME

Gibson had reportedly become moody, even depressed, during his later years. Some wondered whether he felt bitter about not getting to play in the major leagues. After all, Gibson was easily the best hitter in black baseball. But because of his skin color, he was not given an opportunity to achieve the fame and financial success that came with playing in the majors. Jackie Robinson played his first MLB game a few months after Gibson's death.

Those close to Gibson said he was not angry, at least not on a day-to-day basis. That is where the last image of him before his death comes in: Gibson laughing with everyone else in the room. *That*, former teammate Ted Page said, was Josh. If he was disappointed about not getting to play in the major leagues, he did not dwell on it for too long. He was having too much fun playing baseball for a living.

> **"I remember my first swing around the American League, the older guys would point out to me, 'That's where Josh Gibson hit one. . . . That's where Josh Gibson hit one.' Well, I know nobody in our league hit them any farther than that."**
>
> —*Boston Red Sox great Ted Williams, 1969*

Page told a story about playing a night game in Pittsburgh. Then the team drove 600 miles (966 km) to play an afternoon game in St. Louis. At the end of that game, the players got in their cars again and drove another 350 miles (563 km) to play a doubleheader in Kansas City. That night, Page and Gibson were sitting on the porch of their hotel when they spotted some boys playing a sandlot game. Page and Gibson got out of their chairs and asked the boys if they could play too.

END OF AN ERA

In some ways, Gibson's death in 1947 foretold the death of the Negro Leagues. Robinson led black players into the major leagues that year. The Negro Leagues were never again as important as they had been during the three previous decades.

Yet over the previous half century, the Negro Leagues showed that the best black players were as good as—and some better than—white major league players. The black players and teams found ways to continue the sport in the face of racism. The Grays and the Crawfords and the Monarchs and all the other teams in black baseball played the game with a flair and excellence that changed baseball forever.

This, then, is perhaps how the Negro Leagues should be remembered: not as a proving ground for those who finally crossed the color line, but as thriving leagues in their own right with some of the greatest teams and players in the history of the game.

Josh Gibson was one of many great black baseball players who never had an opportunity to play in the major leagues.

TIMELINE

1884: Truly the First

Jackie Robinson is credited with breaking MLB's color line in 1947. However, the first black major leaguer actually debuted 63 years earlier—before the color line was drawn. Catcher Moses Fleetwood Walker played 42 games for the American Association's Toledo Blue Stockings in 1884, hitting .263 and scoring 23 runs.

1931: Great Team, or Greatest Team?

There is much debate over which Negro Leagues teams and players were the best. One survey of black historians in 2007 named the 1931 Homestead Grays as the best ever. That team featured five future Hall of Famers. Another one of the Negro Leagues' all-time great teams was the 1935 Pittsburgh Crawfords. That squad also featured five future Hall of Famers.

1859

The Henson Base Ball Club faces the Weeksville Unknowns in the first known baseball game between all-black teams.

1900

No black players are left in Major League Baseball.

1920

The first Negro National League is formed.

1933

The second Negro National League is formed.

1935: East-West Classic

The 1935 East-West All-Star Game was an instant classic. The East team took a 4–0 lead only to have the West come back to tie it. Then the East took an 8–4 lead in the 10th inning only to have the West again come back to tie it. The West finally won on a play involving three Negro Leagues greats. Slugger George "Mule" Suttles hit a three-run homer in the bottom of the 11th, driving in James "Cool Papa" Bell and Josh Gibson.

1937

The Negro American League is formed.

1937: All-Stars Anywhere

In search of more money, several top Negro League players—including Cool Papa Bell and Josh Gibson as well as pitcher Satchel Paige—went to the Dominican Republic in 1937 to play for Trujillo's Dragones, a team backed by that country's dictator. Not surprisingly, they won the league title.

1941

Negro Leagues popularity soars while the United States fights in World War II.

1947

Jackie Robinson plays for the Brooklyn Dodgers.

1948: An End and a Start

The 1948 season was significant in that it was the NNL's last season and also the last Negro World Series. However, one of the players on the Negro World Series runner-up Birmingham Black Barons was a 17-year-old named Willie Mays. He went on to become arguably the greatest outfielder in MLB history.

1971

Leroy "Satchel" Paige is inducted into the National Baseball Hall of Fame.

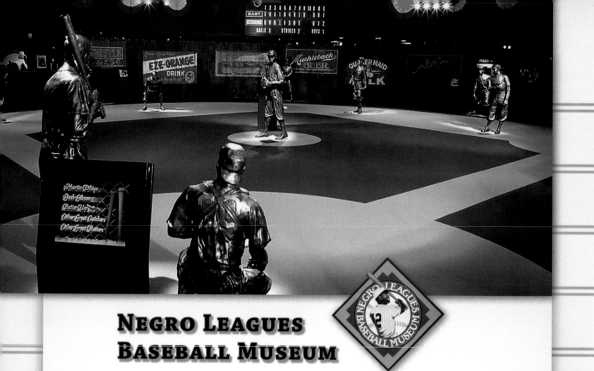

NEGRO LEAGUES BASEBALL MUSEUM

1616 East 18th Street
Kansas City, MO 64108-1610
816-221-1920
www.nlbm.com

The Negro Leagues Baseball Museum preserves the history of Negro Leagues baseball through interactive exhibits, films, photos, sculptures, and artifacts. The museum does not serve as a hall of fame for black baseball. Because the sport is no longer segregated, the Negro Leagues Baseball Museum recognizes the National Baseball Hall of Fame in Cooperstown, New York, as the shrine for all of baseball's greatest players.

The museum opened in 1994 and moved into a new 10,000-square-foot space in 1997. It is located in the historic 18th & Vine Jazz District, a traditional center for black culture in Kansas City. The Paseo YMCA building, where the Negro National League was founded in 1920, is nearby.

GLOSSARY

attendance
> The number of fans who attend a game, a series, or a season.

barnstorming
> When a team travels around and faces various opponents rather than playing in a traditional league.

color line
> An unwritten barrier within MLB that prevented black players from playing in the majors until Jackie Robinson joined the Brooklyn Dodgers in 1947.

contract
> A binding agreement between two parties. In baseball, a contract covers things such as salary and how many years a player will play for a team.

discrimination
> Treating people differently based on prejudice.

exhibition
> A game in which the teams play to develop skills and promote the sport rather than for a competitive advantage.

inducted
> Formally added.

integration
> The act of unifying things that had been kept apart.

pennant
> A flag. In baseball, it symbolizes that a team has won its league championship.

Purple Heart
> A military honor awarded to those who were killed or injured while serving for the United States.

segregated
> When groups of people are legally separated from each other.

semiprofessional
> A level below professional in which players are paid but not enough to survive on as a full-time job.

FOR MORE INFORMATION

Select Bibliography

Dixon, Phil. *The Monarchs 1920–1938: Featuring Wilber "Bullet" Rogan, the Greatest Ballplayer in Cooperstown*. Sioux Falls, SD: Mariah Press, 2002.

Hogan, Lawrence D. *Shades of Glory*. Washington DC: National Geographic Society, 2006.

Holway, John. *The Complete Book of the Negro Leagues: The Other Half of Baseball History*. Fern Park, FL: Hastings House Publishers, 2001.

O'Neil, Buck. *I Was Right on Time*. New York: Simon & Schuster, 1996.

Peterson, Robert. *Only the Ball Was White*. New York: Oxford University Press, 1970.

Further Readings

Nelson, Kadir. *We Are the Ship: The Story of Negro League Baseball*. New York: Jump at the Sun/Hyperion Books for Children, 2008.

Smith, Charles R. *Stars in the Shadows: The Negro League All-Star Game of 1934*. New York: Atheneum, 2012.

Sturm, James, and Rich Tommaso. *Satchel Paige: Striking Out Jim Crow*. New York: Jump at the Sun, 2007.

Weatherford, Carole Boston. *A Negro League Scrapbook*. Honesdale, PA: Boyds Mills Press, 2005.

Withers, Ernest C. *Negro League Baseball*. New York: Harry N. Abrams, 2004.

Web Links

To learn more about the Negro Leagues, visit ABDO Publishing Company online at **www.abdopublishing.com**. Web sites about the Negro Leagues are featured on our Book Links page. These links are routinely monitored and updated to provide the most current information available.

Places to Visit

Highmark Legacy Square

PNC Park
115 Federal Street
Pittsburgh, PA 15212
412-325-4700
http://pittsburgh.pirates.mlb.com/pit/community/legacysquare.jsp
Located just outside the Pittsburgh Pirates' PNC Park, Highmark Legacy Square offers interactive exhibits dedicated to preserving the history of the Negro Leagues, including the local Homestead Grays and Pittsburgh Crawfords.

National Baseball Hall of Fame

25 Main Street
Cooperstown, NY 13326
888-HALL-OF-FAME
www.baseballhall.org
This hall of fame and museum highlights the greatest players and moments in the history of baseball. Over the last several decades, several former Negro Leaguers have been inducted and enshrined here.

INDEX

About the Author: Paul Hoblin has written several sports books. He has an MFA from the University of Minnesota.